The Key to Fruitful Christian Service

by
J. B. Toews

25¢ each
5 for $1.00
(quantity prices on request)

order from

Back to the Bible Publishers
Box 233   Lincoln 1, Nebraska

Printed in the United States

CONTENTS

CONTENTS

J. B. Toews was born and raised in Southern Russia. His home was one where Christ was loved and served. His father was a minister of the gospel. The family saw much suffering and privation, especially after the Communists came to power. In the providence of God, the Toews family eventually made its escape and began life afresh in Canada. J. B. Toews completed his education in Canada and the United States.

He has served in the Bible school and college field and as a pastor both in Canada and the United States. He is at present a missionary executive with responsibilities that take him to many countries.

The messages in this book were delivered at a Back to the Bible prayer conference. They were recorded on tape and are presented very much as they were given. The informal style and language of the spoken message have been preserved.

These messages proved to be very heart searching in their results in that conference. We trust they shall be equally so in this form. Only Christ embodies all truth and expresses it in the richness of its fulness and depth. Yet in His sovereign mercy, he takes one of His vessels and speaks through him certain aspects of truth more forcefully and effectively than He does through some others. It is very evident that the matters dealt with in this volume are not theoretical, but are based on the Word and come from practical experience in God's school of discipline and suffering.

We trust that these devotional meditations will lead many of God's people to place a higher value on service for Christ and to seek a closer walk with Him than ever before.

—Theodore H. Epp

Chapter I

THE BASIS OF THE MINISTRY

This series of meditations will center on the subject matter found in the fourth chapter of II Corinthians. Our subject title is introduced for us in the first two verses which read: "Therefore seeing we have this ministry, as we have received mercy, we faint not; But have renounced the hidden things of dishonesty, not walking in craftiness, nor handling the Word of God deceitfully; but by manifestation of the truth commending ourselves to every man's conscience in the sight of God."

Bible students know that II Corinthians is Paul's defense of his apostleship. Considerable opposition to the ministry of Paul and the ministry of the church had grown through a legalistic sect which had entered the Corinthian church. Paul found it necessary to answer the accusations made by this group which sought to counteract the gospel of grace through their emphasis on legalistic forms. In the first three chapters the apostle gives a general analysis of the ministry. He speaks of the provisions of the ministry, the call to the ministry, the character of the ministry, and then the transcending glory of that ministry in comparison to the ministry of Moses. The third chapter sums up this section by showing how much more glorious is the New Testament ministry to that of the Old.

A very significant fact to observe as we begin this study is that Paul speaks of the responsibility of the ministry as not belonging to himself alone but to all the servants of God. In only a few instances does he make a personal reference. These are easily seen because the personal pronoun is in the singular. Again and again he uses the plural pronoun "we." The very first phrase in the passage just cited is a good example: "Therefore seeing we have this ministry."

Christian service is carried on by many persons, not by just one person. It is a corporate function, not an individual function. All believers have a part in the great program of the ministry of God. Each one has a distinct share in it. God does choose certain individuals to perform specific aspects of that service, but when we speak in terms of "the ministry," we must think of it in the sense of all believers working together toward one goal. I can never set my service apart from its relationship to the responsibilities which all of God's co-workers share in meeting the obligations of the Christian ministry.

Take for example, the ministry of the Back to the Bible Broadcast. It is a world-wide ministry but not that of one man, or two, or three. It is a corporate ministry where each individual in the organization constitutes a vital part of the ministry. Here is a case were God has entrusted a specific service to a large body of people on whose individual shoulders He has placed the responsibility for that service.

The same principle holds with reference to believers in a local church. All bear a vital relationship to each other and share the responsibility of the ministry in their locality. Through helping other Christian organizations such as the Back to the Bible Broadcast or through supporting their own missionaries these churches extend the scope of their ministry. But the point we are making is that the responsibilities of the ministry fall not only upon individuals but upon all of God's people, and that all of us bear a vital relationship to one another with regard to these matters.

There is a divine order in the arrangement of the New Testament books. In Romans we see the work of God in salvation. In I Corinthians it is the work of God in sanctification, and in II Corinthians God's work through us in service. So here in II Corinthians we are dealing with the third level in God's relationship to His redeemed. There is first of all salvation for men, then sanctification in men, and now His divine manifestation through men.

Another question must be raised and answered before we go into an extended analysis of our subject. What is the focal point of Christian service? By observing many Christians today one would think that it was activity. But such is not the case. The focal point in the gospel ministry is the manifestation and the glorification of God in Christ Jesus through His redeemed people. This is the evaluation we must place upon our position in the Christian ministry to which God has called us. We are not all gifted alike but all the various endowments have their vital place in the corporate function of the responsibility of the Christian ministry.

One more observation needs to be made before we take up the study of these introductory verses. God's purposes in working through the individual member of the incorporate body of which we speak will be limited if that individual's spiritual qualifications are not what they should be. Thus the over-all work of God that He has entrusted to His church will be hindered, so vital is the place of each individual in meeting the corporate responsibility of the ministry.

A Strange Introduction

It is a very simple yet remarkable approach that the Apostle Paul makes to the subject of the ministry. There is very little theology needed in order to grasp the truth to which he refers in this passage.

He begins with the word, "therefore," which points back to the first three chapters in which he has outlined the glory and the victory and the cost of the ministry. Now he says that because of the greatness and glory of that ministry "as we have received mercy, we faint not." This is a strange introduction. This is the premise to the ministry.

The mercy of God to usward is the key to this verse. The Christian ministry rests in the revelation of the manifestation of the mercy of God to us.

What do we understand mercy to be? Quite often grace and mercy are used interchangeably as though they meant exactly the same thing. There is a close relationship between them, of course, but when the Bible speaks of grace it speaks of the unmerited favor of God. When it speaks of mercy it makes special reference to the unworthiness of those who receive divine grace. Mercy is the unmerited favor of God to an unworthy person, one who set himself against the will of God, and who in his natural heart is in a constant condition of rebellion against God.

So then in speaking here of mercy, Paul is pointing out the fact that we are totally unworthy of God's favor—yet it is to us He has extended the privilege of a divine ministry. Paul fully realized his own unworthiness and that of all of us. He makes it plain that our part in the gospel ministry is not given to us because we have responded to the grace of God but because we are the objects of the divine mercy.

As you study the Word of God, you cannot help but be struck by the fact that one of the greatest dangers to those whom God has called to a special ministry is their forgetting they were objects of mercy. When they forget where they were found by the mercy of God, and the pit from which they were rescued, they blunder most grievously.

Look what happened to David when he forgot the place from which God took him before He elevated him to the kingship. These words, "As he walked on the roof of the king's palace," are significant in that tragic chapter in his life in which Bathsheba played so significant a part. David, in the glory of his position, forgot that he had been a man picked up from herding sheep by the mercy of God and elevated to the rulership of Israel. He betrayed the confidence placed in him and thereby disqualified himself for the sacred ministry to which God had appointed him.

Israel's sad failures can be traced to the same root problem. Through that nation God was to be gloriously manifested to the world. For that purpose He gave them His revelation from heaven and the impressive ceremonies of the temple worship. But again and again they forgot what they were when God called them and brought them into this special relationship with Himself. They forgot that they were objects of mercy.

It is a refreshing contrast to see in the writings of the Apostle Paul how he was always conscious of what he was and what he had done before he was saved, and how in mercy God had called him into the fellowship of the gospel ministry. Paul could never forget that he had persecuted the Church of Jesus Christ, and that God was merciful and gave him a place of service.

We are suitable or acceptable for Christian service only insofar as we remind ourselves that we have been called into that privileged position by the mercy of God.

A number of years ago I was called to the pastorate of a large church in a Western state. At the time I received the call I was president of a Bible college and so, of course, had to resign that position in order to accept the responsibilities of the pastorate.

When I arrived to take up my new responsibilities I found that a considerable amount of publicity had been given to me because I was taking over the pastorate of the largest church in that part of the country. The press made a great deal over the fact that I was coming. When I arrived at my destination I found on my desk a copy of a newspaper with my picture in it and a large write-up concerning me. I turned on the radio and heard the announcer give the title for my first message at the church. This was all in keeping with the present trend in our country of giving a large "build-up" to certain persons in leadership of one kind or another. But I am afraid it is a practice that is bringing the entire gospel ministry into disrepute.

When I reached my church office the secretary who had been awaiting my arrival, handed me a slip of paper on which was the address of an old lady who wanted the new pastor to call on her as soon as possible. I wondered what the problem might be and asked the secretary, "Is the lady very sick?"

"No," she said, "she isn't."

"Well," I asked, "who is she?"

"I don't know much about her," was the answer, "but she expects you to come and call on her before you preach your first sermon on Sunday."

I thought the message rather urgent, so decided to make the call.

I found the lady on a little ranch some miles out of town. She was hard of hearing and at first it was difficult for me to make her understand that I was the new pastor. When she finally understood who I was she said, "Well, you come in here." I went inside and sat down in the humble home in which she lived.

She looked at me for a while and then began to speak to me in low Dutch and said, "I want to know who you really are."

Of course I told her I was the new pastor.

"Yes, but where do you come from?"

"Well, I came from a college in Canada. I was president of that college."

"No, I don't mean that, whether you were president or not president. I mean where did you come from? Who was your mother?"

I answered, "My mother was Margaret Jantz."

Then she wanted to know where the Jantzes lived and I told her that they lived back in the old country, and gave her the name of the place my family came from.

She said, "That couldn't be the Jantz that had the windmill at the end of the village?"

I said, "Yes, that was my grandfather."

Again she asked the name of my mother which I told her. Then she said, "I thought you were somebody, but now I find out you are nobody but Jantz' Margaret's John. Since you come from there, you don't have very much that you can brag about. I know where you come from."

The radio and newspaper publicity was in marked contrast to this little lady's greeting. God picked out an old mother living on a ranch to help a pastor see his ministry in the right perspective. I had little to brag about. I was the grandson of a godly man, but a man who came from a humble background. To her way of thinking I was not much of anything.

Her standard of evaluation, of course, was economic. But its spiritual lesson was not lost upon me. It is vital for each one of us in the gospel ministry to remember we are there by the mercy of God. It helps us to keep our sense of values straight by remembering the spiritual poverty out of which God picked us.

While in Europe, I made several visits to two of the terrible extermination camps where the Nazis had destroyed many thousands of Jewish people. As I searched my mind and heart for something to strengthen me in the face of these awful atrocities, there suddenly came to me the thought that by a miracle of grace, our brother Richard Wolff of the Back to the Bible Broadcast was not included among the camp's victims. I had heard his voice over the radio that very morning in French and also in German. God is using that ministry all over Europe, but the man behind it is there only because of God's mercy. If you think of our dear brother Epp as the director of the Back to the Bible Broadcast and his relationship to the world-wide ministry of the gospel, you will see the same truth. It is only God's mercy that He picked him up at a filling station and said, "Come here, my son. I have a work for you to do." Let us be honest in the sight of God. That was mercy.

The entire foundation of the gospel ministry is the deep inward consciousness that as we have received mercy, we have this ministry. This is true no matter where our service may be or what it may entail.

Our passage tells us, "Therefore ... as we have received mercy, we faint not." Thus we see that continued dependence on the mercy of God keeps us from fainting in the exercise of the ministry. In other words, this mercy keeps us from becoming despondent through fear and from growing weary in our work. We will discharge our personal responsibilities to this ministry only to the extent that we see we are dependent upon the mercy of God. This is the first step in a spiritual and productive ministry, but it is an essential one.

Honesty in Character and Practice

The second step is given in the second verse. Here the apostle tells us, "But (we) have renounced the hidden things of dishonesty, not walking in craftiness, nor handling the word of God deceitfully; but by manifestation of the truth commending ourselves to every man's conscience in the sight of God." Honesty in character and in practice is a second basis in the gospel ministry.

We should underline the word "hidden" in this verse. The hidden things of dishonesty has reference in particular to those things which cannot be discovered by other people. It does not speak of dishonesty in finances for they are on the surface where they can be more readily perceived. The hidden things of dishonesty concern the inward motivations of the heart. They have to do with purpose.

God is very much concerned that we renounce all dishonest things. These enter into the ministry when we take a professional attitude toward our responsibilities and discharge our share as a matter of routine. It is dishonest for us to claim to be constantly serving our God when the deep consciousness of our personal relationship to Him is lost, and we do things simply because they are expected of us.

In my work at present I am associated with more than 200 missionaries scattered over the face of the earth. Theirs is no easy task. Missionary work has been greatly idealized in these last years, but no one knows better than the missionaries or those who work with them what difficulties they have to face. But below the surface of glamour and glory that attaches to missions, there are titanic struggles and battles against the forces of Satan. The evil one would seek to bring in dishonesty in character, in purpose, in motivation— all this remember, in addition to the problems of new environments and languages and customs and living conditions to which missionaries must learn to adjust. This tends to put Christian workers on the defensive And that raises the following question: It is because we are so much on the defensive these days against the attacks of the enemy that we are not able to take the offensive and make a greater impact with the gospel for Christ?   .

Remember, our passage is dealing with a corporate relationship not only an individual relationship. There can be an inner dishonesty in such a relationship which may never be discovered by men, though it would be recognized if it were brought to the surface.

Paul elaborates on this a little more when he speaks of "not walking in craftiness." Craftiness is hidden deception. The surface appearance may be good, but deep down under that surface there may be motives other than the one which seeks the glory of the Son of God. God is a holy God and will accept no other motive in service. Paul was aware of this when he said, "We have renounced the hidden things of dishonesty."

May I ask you a question? What is your motive

17

in serving God? Perhaps you think I am becoming very personal in probing beneath the surface, but remember that we battle against the forces of darkness which infiltrate today the most secret chambers of the gospel ministry. The glory of God is the only good reason and motive for serving Him. God does not need men and women who enter His service in one way or another with an alternative motive. This is true whether we are in places of leadership in God's work, or not. It applies to us regardless of our place and position of service for Christ. All God's people are His witnesses. What motivates us in our service? It is right here that the hidden things of dishonesty show up, and these must be renounced before the true glory of the ministry can shine forth.

Again we are taken forward a step in this examination when Paul says, "Not handling the Word of God deceitfully." You may not be a preacher or a teacher or a writer but in one way or another you contribute to the total ministry of the gospel of Jesus Christ. How then does Paul's statement apply to us?

We deceive ourselves when we pretend a degree of holiness which does not really exist in our innermost heart. It is a shocking thing to use the Word of God deceitfully.

In concluding this portion Paul says, "Commending ourselves to every man's conscience in the sight of God." So sure was Paul of the purity of his ministry that he asserts here it stood up under the censorship of God. The manifestation of the truth of Jesus Christ through Paul was such that the apostle was able to say, "We commend ourselves to every man's conscience." His ministry having stood the test of God's scrutiny, he could speak of it unashamedly before men.

When I read that statement I squirmed inwardly like a worm before God. According to human evaluation, which in this realm may be very gentle, we perhaps all would feel we had done right. But it is another matter to have our lives evaluated by the penetrating insight of the holy, omniscient, and eternal God.

During my college days I had a roommate who had been taught to drink only rain water. When he came to school he insisted on following this practice even in the dining room. One day in the chemical laboratory he received an assignment to make an analysis of rain water. He and I worked together on the problem. He put a drop of rain water on a glass slide and placed it under a microscope. I noticed that he quickly removed the slide and polished it most carefully. Then he added another drop of rain water. Again he looked at it through the microscope. He removed the glass slide and polished it, added another drop of water, and looked again. This he repeated four or five times. I asked him what was wrong. He answered, "There are horrible things in this water." Then he added, "This must be stale water. I'm going to get some different water."

He found some fresh rain water and started the experiment all over again, but the result was the same.

When we went into the dining room at noon, he left his glass of rain water untouched. One of the boys said to him, "What about your water? Why did you not drink it?"

He answered, "I could not after I saw what was in it."

The point is that we do not really see ourselves as we are. When God puts us under His microscope there is nothing that remains hidden. Only by the grace of God can we "commend ourselves to every man's conscience in the sight of God."

The things we have considered so far constitute the basis of the Christian ministry. We have found that the service of which Paul speaks carries a corporate responsibility, that is, it includes all believers—all truly born-again ones. We have found that this ministry rests in the mercy of God, and that even our privilege of sharing in it is based on God's mercy expressed in our redemption and then in our call to face this responsibility.

We have also considered the necessity of honesty before God. We can commend ourselves to every man's conscience only as we ourselves are right in God's sight. Those two facts, then, that all of God's people bear responsibility to this ministry and that they live in such a manner that their lives commend the gospel to those around them, constitutes the only basis of the Christian ministry. We hear much today of things that are relative rather than absolute. We cannot deal with God and His truth on a relative basis. It must be on an absolute basis. Divine truth is absolute in its inner character and application. The ministry is not founded on men's opinions or the fallen character of men, but in the revelation of God and the absolute holiness of His person.

Chapter II

THE ISSUES OF THE MINISTRY

The inspired apostle lay down the issues of the ministry in the following verses: "But if our gospel be hid, it is hid to them that are lost: In whom the god of this world hath blinded the minds of them which believe not, lest the light of the glorious gospel of Christ, who is the image of God, should shine unto them. For we preach not ourselves, but Christ Jesus the Lord; and ourselves your servants for Jesus' sake" (II Cor. 4:3-5).

Before we can have any proper evaluation of a specific Christian relationship, it is necessary that we know what issues are involved in it. In order to determine where we are at any particular moment with reference to our geographic location, we must know the main directions of north, south, east, and west. It is equally essential that we keep our sense of values and direction in our spiritual relationships.

We must have a very keen consciousness of the issues which are involved in the Christian ministry. The basic ones are given in this passage and on reading them we are brought to the realization that the Christian ministry is more than a job or an occupation. It distresses me when those in what we call full-time Christian service put their ministry on the same level with a profession or an occupation. It is far more than that. A study of the life of the Apostle Paul will disclose that his ministry was to him the central purpose of his salvation.

A careful reading of the twenty-sixth chapter of Acts where Paul made his defense before Agrippa provides this statement made by the Lord to Paul: "For this very purpose I appeared unto thee that thou mayest be a witness unto the Gentiles." It makes a tremendous difference whether we receive an assignment because we have been redeemed or we are redeemed for an assignment. When we say we have been redeemed for a purpose then we notice that the assignment is the heart and the center of our redemption. That primary purpose must not be made a secondary thing. We must remember that we have not been made ministers of the gospel of Christ because we have been redeemed, but we were redeemed in order that we might perform a ministry.

If our viewpoint is that we minister because we have been saved, the emphasis is laid upon our choice. But if we believe that we were redeemed in order that we might minister, then the prerogative lies with God and not with us. It is not we who are extending a favor to God when we accept a part in this ministry, but God who has condescended to give us such a part.

We were redeemed for the purpose of the ministry. That is the divine aspect. This is God's viewpoint, not man's. And it is from this divine aspect that we view the issues of the ministry as revealed in these verses.

Our Ministry Affects Eternal Destinies

Let us look at verses three and four again and we will not be able to escape the conclusion that, as we witness of our God and the salvation He has provided, we affect the eternal destinies of men and women. "But if our gospel be hid, it is hid to them that are lost: In whom the god of this world has blinded the minds of them that believe not, lest the light of the glorious gospel of Christ, who is the image of God, should shine unto them." Our ministry enters the very center of the spiritual conflict depicted here: "But if our gospel be hid, it is hid to them that are lost." Connect this with what Paul said in the previous verse: "But have renounced the hidden things of dishonesty, not walking in craftiness, nor handling the word of God deceitfully; but by manifestation of the truth commending ourselves to every man's conscience in the sight of God." Here he tells us that his ministry was performed with such honesty and truthfulness that in the sight of God Himself he was able to commend himself to every man's conscience. Consequently if the gospel was hid, it was not due to any fault of Paul's.

He emphasized the same truth in the Book of Acts when he said, "I am pure of the blood of all men." Think of the extent of the meaning of that statement. Though his ministry stood in the center of the spiritual conflict which influences the eternal destinies of millions of souls, he had so conducted himself by manifesting to the world the reality of the living and saving Christ that he was free from the blood of all men. Can we say that with reference to our own testimony? Is the risen Christ, who is able to save, seen in us to the extent that those who meet us are brought face to face with these eternal issues because of us?

This first great issue of our ministry shows us that we enter into the center of the spiritual conflict which influences the destiny of untold numbers of souls. We are therefore in a ministry which constitutes the conflict of eternity. This we must never lose sight of.

We must not think of our service or ministry in the sense of our witnessing for the Lord Jesus only. It is more than a matter of testifying to the benefits that we have received in Christ. We must realize that we are in the thick of the conflict between light and darkness. This battle consciousness must never be lost by us. The moment we lose it, that moment we become ineffective in the ministry to which we have been called.

Sometime ago I found it necessary to travel from Vienna, Austria, to Frankfort-on-Main in Germany. During one part of the journey an officer of the United States occupation army in Germany was in the same compartment with me. We conversed together and during the course of our talk I said to him, "Officer, tell me, what do you consider to be the most essential part of your responsibility in the occupation forces?"

He was quiet for a little bit and then answered, "The most essential part of my job is to keep our men battle conscious." This was rather a striking statement so I asked him to explain what he meant.

"Well," he said, "it is not a shooting war. Nevertheless, we are only a few minutes away from the nearest of the enemy's bases." He continued, "In a few minutes they could drop an atom bomb on us and cripple our battle ability." "So," he continued, "to constantly maintain that alertness and consciousness, even though the guns are not firing, is the most difficult task we have."

To say in our Christian ministry that we are serving the Lord does not really get down to the great issue in this matter. The real issue is in the tremendous spiritual conflict which could be the deciding factor in the destiny of millions of souls. This is the great matter we must ever be conscious of in order to keep basic issues before us. No matter what aspect of service may be ours or in whatever locality we serve, this is the issue with which we are dealing.

The central issue in this relationship is not merely a pious response to the grace that we have received through the mercy of the Lord. Such a mediocrity of concept in the Christian ministry we need to be redeemed from. The ministry in which we are engaged influences the destiny of souls. Their choice with regard to it decides whether they shall spend eternity in heaven or in hell. The moment we lose the consciousness of this essential issue we lose the effectiveness of our ministry.

Some years ago a minister of the gospel was traveling in a car; his wife and young son, a boy eight years old were with him in the front seat. They were traveling through hilly country and the road was wet. A car going in the same direction passed them at a terrific rate of speed. As they came over a hill they saw the car again just as the young man driving it lost control, and it turned across the highway. Coming from the other direction was another car also traveling at a high speed, and it crashed into this first one. In a moment the highway was littered with debris and with the torn, broken bodies of the occupants of both cars.

The little boy saw the catastrophe. He became pale as a sheet. He did not speak a word the rest of the way. In fact, none of them did. They had nothing to say.

When they arrived at their destination the parents were disturbed at their son's nervousness. They put him to bed. Ten o'clock came, then eleven, then twelve, then after twelve, and still the boy remained awake.

His father sat beside him trying to calm him, and said, "Sweetheart, won't you try to sleep?"

Suddenly the little fellow's emotions overcame him. He burst into tears and said, "Daddy, when people die, can we sleep?"

The ministry of the apostle always had the issue of the eternal destiny of men and women at its center. The moment we lose that consciousness we have lost the basic qualification for Christian service. Can we sleep when people die? It is of that the apostle speaks when he says, "If our gospel be hid, it is hid to them that are lost."

He then goes on to say, "In whom the god of this world hath blinded the eyes of them which believe not, lest the light of the glorious gospel of Christ, who is the image of God, should shine unto them." Notice that he does not say that we can determine the eternal destiny of man. There is a responsibility which lies with the individual himself, because the Scripture says, "Them which believe not." Their eyes are blinded by the god of this world, but in the end the full responsibility lies with the individual who refuses to respond to the gospel appeal. Do not, however, overlook the fact that our ministry is to present the occasion or occasions whereby the people who are now blinded can make the proper decision for Christ. If they reject Him, the responsibility is theirs.

I have as one of my friends an outstanding surgeon. He is a deeply spiritual, Bible-believing man, and has a great heart for missions. Of late he has not been well, and when I visited with him not long ago I conversed with him freely over the possible cause of his illness. He is a comparatively young man and under ordinary circumstances ought to have good health. In our conversation he suddenly said with emotion, "Mr. Toews, the problem with me is that in the surgical field one is always dealing with the issues of life and death. It is having to deal with this constant burden that has broken me down."

"Well, Doctor," I said, "you are doing your best, so surely it is not your responsibility since you do your best, is it?" He turned to me and said, "Why is it that you do not think that way in your preaching?"

He was right. I dare not think that way with reference to the ministry. When we lose the deep consciousness that people under our ministry are deciding for life or death, for eternal life or eternal destruction, then we lose that inward spiritual

27

qualification that makes for an effective ministry irrespective of what area we may labor in. To one the service may be the playing of an organ, to another that of singing, to another that of writing letters, still another that of giving out tracts, or in whatever way the cause of Christ may be served. But this issue must grip us with increasing force if we are to deal effectively in these matters. Should this grasp the hearts of God's people in America today our entire nation would feel the impact of it; and the consciousness of the holiness of God would humble men and women the country over. That is the number one issue.

The consciousness of this truth makes me wish that I could preach every time in the Spirit as though it were the last message I would ever be able to preach to dying souls. The urgency and the seriousness of mind that this issue presses upon us should cause us to determine that, whatever we do in our ministry for the Lord, it will be done with the hope of pointing some soul to life in Christ.

We Preach Christ, Not Ourselves

The second issue in these verses deals with the message of the ministry. "For we preach not ourselves, but Christ Jesus the Lord; and ourselves your servants for Jesus' sake." The words, "we preach not ourselves," are the significant ones here. The context of this expression does not speak only of the contents of the message of the inward motivation in our giving out the message. We do not preach ourselves. We do not have ourselves in mind when we preach. We are not presenting ourselves to men and women but the Lord Jesus Christ. You will also notice that the expression, "Jesus, the Lord," does not say "a Lord," but "the Lord." There is an absoluteness in that statement.

One of the greatest difficulties in the ministry is to keep from protruding ourselves into the foreground. When we are guilty of this we seek self-gratification through the ministry. Some find delight that they can earn their livelihood in working for the Lord, and at the same time have a part in that over-all world-wide ministry. But do you realize that it is from this level that all the bickering and dissatisfaction and rivalry arises in the ranks of Christian workers? The deepest grief in the ministry today is the protrusion of human personalities where Christ should be glorified.

This is a hard word to utter, but as long as we seek self-gratification and self-reward in the ministry, it would be better for us not to be in it. Indeed that is a hard thing to say, but we must become hard with ourselves. We are not here to serve ourselves. We are not to be looking to the ministry for favors which gratify us. We serve Christ Jesus the Lord. And where the ministry is placed completely under His Lordship, then this issue is being fully met. We serve not men; we serve not ourselves; we serve the Lord.

We place a halo around missionaries and around ministers of the gospel. Yet they possibly, as no others, are subject to testing along this line. These we consider high levels of gospel ministry, but it is on these same high levels that we see some of the greatest defeats.

We Are Servants of One Another

We do not preach ourselves but Christ Jesus the Lord the apostle tells us, and then he adds, "And ourselves your servants for Jesus' sake." We acknowledge the Lordship of Christ and servitude to man. It is this latter which tests us to the core. The ministry demands or requires that we be servants unto those to whom we minister. It is sometimes a hard battle for us to accept the Lordship of Him who is Lord of lords and King of kings; but that is not as humiliating to us as being a servant of others for Jesus' sake.

To be subordinate to one another is not easy. It calls for the surrender of our independence. The core of the battle in Eden in which Adam and Eve engaged was a question of subordination on the one hand or of independence on the other. When Satan tempted Eve and said, "Thou shalt not surely die but shall be as gods, knowing good and evil," he held before her the allurement of independence in preference to being subordinate to God. That was the central issue in man's fall.

Somehow that same issue enters again into the Christian ministry. This is where many of us find our greatest difficulty. We recognize we must subordinate ourselves to God, but to do so includes subordination to man. The test of our subordination to God is found in our subordination to man.

Do you know that the greatest destructive force in the Christian ministry today is the unwillingness of God's servants to serve one another? For any of us to stand in leading positions and have men subordinate to us in Christian organizations puts our spiritual qualities to the test. For one to be a superior in an organization without the attitude of being a servant to the people of God is causing untold difficulties in Christian circles. There is this inward rebellion against being a servant that brings such deep grievance to the heart of the Holy Spirit. We do not want to be servants to our fellow believers. Yet Paul says that we are servants, not for men's sake, however, but for Jesus' sake.

I know a Christian home in which the father is a leader in certain Christian circles. It was necessary for that father to be gone a great deal from that home, and not being able to afford two cars the boys in the family had to do a good deal of walking when the father was away.

One day one of the boys made definite plans for the use of the family car since the father was at home at that particular time. But he found that when he wanted it, the father had to have it for the ministry. He came to his father's study and said, "Dad, I'm beginning to wonder, does the ministry mean that other people have to run you, and that you have to be a servant to all the people?"

The father was silent for a moment and then said, "Son, you have hit it exactly right."

The boy was disturbed over it and said to his father, "Dad, then I never want to be a minister."

The father answered, "Son, God will never use you, then."

A few days later the boy came back to his father and said, "I'm sorry, Dad, for what I said."

Do you realize that the Lord Jesus Christ has given us two great commandments and one is that we love one another? What degree of love is asked for here? "Even as I have loved you," is what our Saviour said. Then He added, "Thereby shall every man know that ye are my disciples, if ye have love one for another." The other commandment is, "Go ye into all the world and preach the gospel to every creature." These are His two commandments and the first deals with servitude.

What great spiritual losses in fruit are being suffered today because we do not want to be servants one to another. Each of us would like to be the greatest. This was true among the disciples when our Lord was preparing to go to the cross. James and John came to Him and asked if they might have the privilege of sitting the one on His right hand and the other on His left. It is this spirit that destroys so much effectiveness in the ministry today.

According to the passage before us, then, there are three issues in the ministry. There is first the consciousness of the affect of our ministry on the eternal destiny of the souls of men. The second great issue is that we preach not ourselves but Christ Jesus the Lord. The third is that we recognize we are not only servants of the Lord, but we are fellow servants of our brethren in Christ. These are the issues of the Christian ministry which must be faced and met if what we do for Christ is to bring honor to Him for time and eternity.

Chapter III

THE VESSELS OF THE MINISTRY

For this section of our study we will concentrate on verses 6 and 7 of II Corinthians 4. They read as follows: "For God, who commanded the light to shine out of darkness, hath shined in our hearts, to give the light of the knowledge of the glory of God in the face of Jesus Christ. But we have this treasure in earthen vessels, that the excellency of the power may be of God, and not of us."

It is the method of God to reveal infinite glory and power through the instrumentality of finite, mortal men. God takes pleasure in using the most insignificant material and most insignificant instruments in order to magnify the grandeur, glory, and beauty of His own Person and redemptive work.

The passage before us dwells specially upon the center of this divine purpose. It is introduced with the statement in verse 6: "For God, who commanded the light to shine out of darkness." This is a reference to the whole purpose of God in giving the divine revelation. It deals with that point in time when God in His infinite wisdom chose to break through the darkness, which had up to that time kept His creative acts hidden. The opening words of the Bible tell us that in the beginning God created the heaven and the earth. It also says that the earth was without form and void and the darkness was on the face of the deep. Then God said, "Let there be light: and there was light." Light penetrated the darkness and the great transactions of God, by which He manifested His glory and power, had their beginning.

This statement goes beyond the creative acts of God in the material universe. It includes the marvelous manifestation of God when He penetrated the darkness of human sin and revealed Himself to lost mankind in the light of the redemptive provision He made in Christ Jesus. So then, in this first statement, "For God, who commanded the light to shine out of darkness," we have a reference to the fact that God through divine revelation has told us how He entered the realm of the finite in such a way that He could be understood and known by men. This revelation goes beyond His provision of a general knowledge for men concerning Himself. It also shows that He entered into personal relationships with men, for it says He has shined into our hearts. This means that God has manifested Himself to my heart and your heart through the gospel.

But God does not stop by speaking of the redemptive purpose in this manifestation of Himself. He uses it to point to the further fact that all God's people, through the wonderful redemption in Christ, have been called to the ministry of the gospel. Let us keep this point clear. We are not speaking of the preacher or the deacon only. We are speaking of the services or ministry committed to God's redeemed people in which each individual has an equal share. The differences between them rests only in the task assigned each one and not in the character of the ministry. This communication of God into our hearts is for the specific purpose of making us vessels through which the wonderful glory of God might shine out to the world. This is made unmistakably clear in verse 7 where we read: "But we have this treasure in earthen vessels, that the excellency of the power may be of God, and not of us."

The Purpose of the Vessel

The sixth verse of the chapter very distinctly gives us the real purpose of our redemption. When asked in our spiritual babyhood what the purpose of our redemption is, we usually say we were redeemed in order to escape the horrors of eternal condemnation. It is a disturbing fact that so many of God's people remain in that state of infancy for such a long time. True, one of the blessings of our redemption is that we escape eternal condemnation, but that is not the purpose of our redemption. The purpose of our redemption is that through us the glory of the infinite God may be demonstrated to the world.

The verse under consideration is not an isolated text on this subject in the Scriptures. For example, in the Gospel of John we find this same truth. Our Saviour said in His high-priestly prayer: "I have glorified thee on the earth (Christ speaks here of the purpose of His coming in the flesh)." His next statement shows how he glorified God. "I have finished the work which thou gavest me to do." Christ manifested the name of God to the people on the earth and gave them His Word. Christ's purpose in coming to make provision for redemption was that the glory of God might be established. The blessing of this redemption rests in the benefits we receive through salvation. But the purpose of this redemption is that the glory of the infinite God might be made known through His provision for the deepest needs of fallen man.

Further on in this chapter the Saviour said, "And the glory which thou gavest me I have given them; that they may be one, even as we are one: I in them, and thou in me, that they may be made perfect in one; and that the world may know that thou hast sent me, and hast loved them, as thou hast loved me" (John 17:22,23). So then, Christ glorified the Father on the earth, and then the glory which God gave Him, Christ gave to us. This glory is to be manifested in the oneness of God's people so that the world may know that God has sent Christ. This glory of God, seen in Christ and then in God's redeemed people, is all for the purpose of attracting the world to Jesus Christ. It is this background of truth which we must grasp when we speak of the vessels of the ministry.

God in His divine grace was desirous of communicating Himself to a lost human race. This He has done through Christ who not only is in heaven, but by His infinite power through the Spirit lives in His people on earth. Also, through their oneness, He indicates to a lost world that God sent Him, and that He is the Son of God. God intends, then, that through vessels of human instrumentality the glory of God in Christ will be communicated to a dying world.

Yet how few of God's people actually occupy themselves with the purpose of their redemption. Too many of them remain in the babyhood of their salvation and occupy themselves with its benefits only.

A little lad climbed into a mulberry tree in order to reach what he thought were the best mulberries. He was stretched out on one of the highest branches when he slipped and landed on the ground, falling flat on his stomach and chest. The breath was knocked out of his body. His father and mother rushed him to a hospital where he later regained consciousness.

When he realized that he had been at the brink of death he said to his father, as his parents sat beside his bed: "Daddy, why didn't God let me die if I was unconscious already?"

"Well," his father replied, "you ask God about that and let Him tell you why."

The next day when the father came to his bedside again the boy said, "Daddy, I did ask God why He didn't take me."

"What did He tell you?" his father asked.

"He told me that He had let me live because He wanted me to do something for Him."

The father replied, "Did God tell you that?"

He answered, "Yes, Daddy, don't you think that God saved my life because He had a purpose for me?"

For the first time in his young life, there had been raised the question of a purpose in life. Will it take a fall from some mulberry tree before we finally ask God why He allows us to live? The answer lies in these Scriptures we are considering.

We live in order that God may use us as vessels
by which to show forth His divine glory. That is
the purpose of our existence. Our emphasis today
is on activity with little said concerning character.
But activity does not answer the need of the cru-
cial age in which we live. Only character can answer that— a character which is the glory of God
in Jesus Christ in you and me. This, then, is the
purpose of the vessel.

The Dependence of the Vessel

From the purpose of the vessel we must take
another step and see the dependence of that vessel.
Remember, it is only a vessel, and it is God
who commanded the light to shine out of darkness, Who has shined in our hearts to give the light
of the knowledge of the glory of God in the face
of Jesus Christ. God commanded that light to
shine and revealed it. He has permitted it to shine
not only into our hearts, but through our hearts
to others.

Thus the vessel is dependent upon the One who
uses it. He must first shine into our hearts before
there can be any reflection from the vessel. Since
the vessel can only reflect that glory, it is dependent upon the continuous communication of
the glory from God. The vessel does not possess
that glory on its own. Only as the glory of Christ
shines in our hearts can it be reflected through us.

In my father's study there was a cross made
with some phosphorous mixture so that it could
absorb light, then reflect it in the darkened room.
This was quite a large cross which my father hung

on a wall where the sun shone on it through the day. In the evening whenever one entered the study he would see the wonderful outline of the illuminated cross.

I was a teen-age boy when I received Christ as my Saviour, and one day following my salvation I was called into my father's study for an interview. Father had been deeply grieved by the behaviour of his son, and when he spoke to me, he made an appeal to the spiritual motivation in my life when he said, "Son, haven't you always confessed that the Lord Jesus lives in your heart?"

"Yes, Daddy," I answered, "I have."

"Well, how is it that something different from the character and reflection of Jesus Christ was revealed in your life today?"

Suddenly pointing to the cross on the wall, he said, "Why does that cross not light up this evening?"

I looked at it and said, "I don't know, Daddy."

"Well," he said, "I'll tell you. The shutters have been closed all day and there has been no sunshine in this room. Because no sunshine has entered this room today, that cross has no light tonight." Then with his deep loving kindness he held my two hands between his hands and with tears in his eyes said, "Son, your shutters have been closed today. No light has come in, and that is why you have no light to let shine out."

Have not the shutters been closed in our present-day Christianity? We are seeking to preach a message without the reflection of the glorious character and beauty of our Christ. We have the vocabulary to fit the message and we repeat the words again and again. But the contents of the message do not have the power of communication except as they are reflected from the character of the glory of the indwelling Christ. Our day and age needs Christ-like men and women. We do not need more preaching, but we need more of God's people in whose life the reflection of Christ is seen.

Many have tried to be Christ-like or to grow into greater Christ-likeness through different kinds of self-effort. They see the need in their lives and seek to meet it by self-determination. Last year when I was teaching a special course in a college, a young woman came to me and said, "Mr. Toews, I have read a book again and again which tells me I should imitate Christ. I have tried to imitate Christ but it doesn't help."

There is a basic weakness in such advice. It is good as far as it goes. It provides a pattern for us to follow, but it is a pattern which we must follow in human weakness. Such a program does not present God's wonderful method whereby He transforms us into Christ-likeness. That can only come through the degree to which we expose ourselves to the grace of the Lord Jesus Christ. That intercommunion of our life with His provides the means whereby more and more of His character is transmitted to us. We reflect the glory and the beauty of Christ through communion, not through resolutions. It is not in what knowledge we may have concerning Christ that brings this change, but the day by day communion with Him. The glory of the gospel of Jesus Christ shining into our hearts brings about Christ-likeness.

Some years ago, I held special services in Los Angeles, and after the last meeting decided to drive home, a distance of some 200 miles. Traffic was heavy on the highway, and the hour was getting late. Finally I found myself behind a bus and could not pass it. Several times I tried to do so, but each time I would see a car coming toward me. The bus driver would not cooperate in any way and was seemingly unconcerned about my desire to pass. Suddenly I was attracted by the wonderful reflection from the rear of the bus. I realized that what I saw were not taillights, but something else. I became so absorbed watching that beautiful display of lights, that I became content to follow the bus. I followed it until it stopped. I got out and asked the driver if there was any trouble. "No," he said, "we have reached the bus depot." I had followed him into the bus depot in Bakersfield, because I was so absorbed in that beautiful reflection. I was a little embarrassed to realize that I had lost my sense of direction, but my curiosity overcame my embarrassment. I said to the driver, "What kind of reflection do you have behind the bus?"

He answered, "We developed that for special safety in night driving. There are several phosphorous strips that we put across the back of the bus, and during sunny days the phosphorous soaks up the sun's rays. These strips are put on in various strengths, so that they give off various degrees of reflection."

So beautiful was that sight that I almost felt sorry I had to leave the bus and drive without it in front of me. Those phosphorous strips on back

41

of the bus reminded me of this passage. The only answer to the world's inner confusion lies in their seeing the reflection of Christ of Whom they have heard so much, but of Whom they have seen so little.

We are dependent vessels. We must be constantly exposed to the inward working of Christ in our lives. We reflect His glory as He shines in our hearts.

Different Kinds of Vessels

God has chosen the most insignificant material out of which to fashion this vessel. It is an earthen vessel made of inexpensive material by which He has chosen to manifest His glory.

In his Second Letter to Timothy the Apostle Paul described the various vessels in the household of God. Some are to honor and some to dishonor (2:20,21). There are vessels of gold and silver which are vessels to honor, and then there are vessels of wood and of earth which are vessels to dishonor. Yet it is the earthen vessels that God has chosen through which to reflect His glory. How marvelous is the grace of God!

If Satan has kept you constantly under the consciousness of your own unworthiness and your incapacities and weaknesses, take courage. He may have used these things to obstruct your growth, but lift up your discouraged spirit and thank God that He is willing to use an earthen vessel.

There is nothing that we have to glory in. God did not choose the gold nor the wood, but the earthen vessel. According to the passage in II

Timothy there is a progression in the transformation of these vessels as they are put to use in the household of God. This is a wonderful thing. As God magnifies His glory in the earthen vessel there comes a process of transformation so that God can speak not only of earthen vessels, but of vessels of wood and silver and gold.

Earthen vessels are prone to crack at the smallest pressure put upon them. In the household of God it seems there are many such parts lying around. From these we need to be redeemed. God chooses us as earthen vessels, but because of a process of divine transformation we do not need to remain in that stage. God wants to transform us into something else, yet there are too many of us who crack as we come in contact in our daily work with others. Someone always irritates us and we are always under tensions. Some of us are earthen pots that have to be tied with string in order to be held together.

The next stage is wooden vessels. This reminds me of an old well that belonged to my grandfather. It was my responsibility to fill a big stock tank with water from the well. The pail I used for that purpose was a wooden one attached to a long rope which, in turn, was slung over a wheel on a pulley. It was a leaky bucket and the water would escape from it so that when I finally pulled the bucket to the surface it was only half full. Then it was necessary for me to take rags and fill up the cracks. Every time I forgot to put the bucket down in the water it was exposed to the sun and would leak worse.

So many of God's people become leaky Christians when they get a little sunshine. They have a great experience in revival or at some Bible conference. They bubble all over and testify of the blessings of God. Then they come into the heat of the sun of daily experience and in a short time they are dried up and their spirituality leaks away. They are wooden vessels unto dishonor.

God chooses earthen vessels but in the process of His divine manifestation He does not expect us to remain as such. Through His marvelous power He wants us to become transformed into vessels of silver and gold; but remember, silver tarnishes easily and has to be constantly wiped in order to be kept shiny.

Occasionally when I have had reason to be abroad I have brought back some silver nicknacks for my wife. But again and again I found that she keeps them out for only a short time then wraps them up and puts them away. I asked her once why she did not keep them out so that we could see them. She told me that they tarnish easily and require a great deal of cleaning. The material itself is good but the outside always needs burnishing. In spite of that drawback they have the added advantage in that they do not break easily as do the earthen vessels.

But then there are vessels of gold and we find that gold stands the test of fire and never tarnishes. How wonderful it is that God chooses an earthen vessel and uses it for His glory, and in the process of reflecting that glory the earthen vessel is transformed into a golden one.

One day on one of our mission fields a native chief came to me and asked for more missionaries.

Then he added, "If you send us missionaries, send us missionaries like Freda" (not her real name). I asked him why he made such a request, and he said, "because she is so much like Jesus, and so much like us."

Our degree of real effectiveness in service will be determined by the degree of Christ-likeness in us. What are you, an earthen vessel that has become a gold vessel? Be honest in this evaluation. Golden vessels are not themselves conscious of the precious material of which they are made through the transforming power of Christ. Our ministry and our influence are dependent upon the character of the vessel. God grant that though we are now earthen vessels we shall become vessels unto honor.

Chapter IV

THE PLACE OF SUFFERING
IN THE MINISTRY

Let us understand clearly that in this study of the ministry we are not dealing with the responsibility of the preacher. In fact, we are not dealing with the responsibility of any specific assignment or area of the ministry in the work of the kingdom of God. What we are dealing with is a spiritual ministry which is part of the inner life of every true, saved child of God. We cannot help but see in the Book of Acts that the secret of the great victory of the Apostolic church was the distribution of responsibility. The onward march of that church did not rest upon the disciples alone. In the fourth chapter we find that the apostles shared with "all" what the high priests and Pharisees said to them. So, you see, there was a distribution of responsibility upon all who were true believers.

Now, on the basis of the Scripture before us in II Corinthians 4, we must deal with the suffering in the ministry. "We are troubled on every side, yet not distressed; we are perplexed, but not in despair; Persecuted, but not forsaken; cast down, but not destroyed; Always bearing about in the body the dying of the Lord Jesus, that the life also of Jesus might be made manifest in our body" (II Cor. 4:8-10).

In order to grasp fully the significance of suffering in the ministry as presented here by the Apostle Paul, we must recognize that all life is conditioned by death. This is a universal principle from which we never can escape. In plant life we find that the seed must die in order to reproduce itself. Furthermore, fruitfulness is also conditioned on suffering.

Some years ago when I made my first visit to California, I stayed with a very fine man of God who had a large orchard. It was the winter season, and since I had never seen how orchards were taken care of during that time of the year, I took a walk one morning to see just what was being done. My host had gone to town on a shopping trip and had left a number of workmen in his orchard cutting and pruning trees. I walked through the rows of trees to see what the workmen were doing, and my heart bled, for I was sure that they were ruining my friend's orchard. I hastily made a telephone call to his brother who lived not too far away and said, "Say, so and so isn't home, and I'm afraid before he comes home, great injury will have been done to his orchard. Why don't you come down and see what these men are doing here."

He lost no time in rushing over in his pickup and asked me what I meant. I took him to the orchard and said, "Look, what they are doing to those trees. They are cutting them down. They will dry up."

He stood there and smiled at me. He said, "If we don't do that, those trees will be very little good to us."

He went with me through the orchard and said, "We have to make these trees bleed if they are to amount to anything."

There were several trees that had not been bearing fruit as the owner thought they should, and his brother showed me what the workmen were doing with them. They had little hatchets and were actually injuring the stems. The workmen were causing them to bleed. They were cutting deep wounds in them. I walked away saying, "These trees are done for."

After two years I went back, and one of the first things I said was, "I want to see those trees that were mistreated so much." My host took me out to see them. They were beautiful and laden with fruit. So you see, fruit-bearing is also conditioned by suffering. Death and suffering are some of the fundamental laws that we must accept into our Christian philosophy if we are to discover the secrets of the marvelous grace of God.

How distinctly these things are taught in the Scriptures. Can we avoid seeing this in John 12:24 where we find the Lord telling us that except a corn of wheat fall into the ground and die, it remaineth alone? But if it dies, it brings forth much fruit. Then again in Luke 9:24 our Saviour sa "Whosoever will save his life shall lose it whosoever shall lose his life for my sake, th shall save it."

How is it that these basic concepts moved so far from the center of th flection of God's people in our da realize that without these we our goal?

Paul's words in this passage in II Corinthians concerning suffering give us a threefold analysis. First of all, we are told of the principle of suffering in the ministry, then of suffering as being a necessity to the ministry, and finally as the greatest benefit in the ministry.

The Principle of Suffering in the Ministry

Paul speaks of being troubled on every side, yet not distressed; perplexed, but not in despair; persecuted, but not forsaken; cast down, but not destroyed. We saw from verse four how that the ministry brings us into the very center of the spiritual conflict. Our opponent is the god of this world who has blinded the minds of them who believe not, lest the light of the glorious gospel of Christ, who is the image of God, should shine unto them. The ministry places us into the very focal point of that spiritual battle. Seeing this, we understand why the apostle says we are troubled on every side. How could there be a battle between light and darkness without suffering and difficulty? Would the archenemy neglect to bring his attack from every angle that he could imagine in order to defeat us in our spiritual ministry? There is a battle-consciousness that must be established if we are to succeed in the ministry. The true ministry is a battle between light and darkness which will bring perplexity and persecution, but never despair and defeat if we enter the conflict in the proper way.

If we have not thought of the ministry as an encounter with the evil one that will produce various battles through which he will seek to disqualify us, we have missed an important factor. We simply have not caught the basic abc's which relate themselves to the principle of suffering in the Christian ministry. Battles under these conditions are necessities. We face perplexities and difficulties of various kinds. The ministry to which God has called us cannot be thought of as a rocking chair ideology which appeals so strongly to this age of ease and comfort and material plenty. Because we stand at the center of the conflict between the forces of light and the forces of darkness, do not expect conquest and comfort at the same time. This is one of the greatest lessons that we in America have to learn.

Satan has succeeded in blinding the eyes of many in our day, so that they think the spiritual battle and conquest can be carried on in circumstances of ease and comfort without any serious exertion and without any real sacrifice. We live in the midst of a great deal of activity and machinery, but somehow there is an increase in spiritual disintegration in the machinery itself. Instead of conquest, it is retreat, because the forces of light have lost the true concept of the requirements of the battle.

As you read the Scriptures and note the progress of God's work from time to time, you will find that no gain was made to His honor and glory without sacrifice. Tribulation and suffering preceded victory. Read the eleventh chapter of Hebrews carefully. There you will see that Moses chose to identify himself with the people of God rather than enjoy the pleasures of Egypt. The Old Testament heroes held a concept of suffering, believing it was an essential and vital part of their testimony.

Paul in writing to his spiritual son, Timothy, said, "If we suffer with Christ, we shall also reign with him." One of the greatest tragedies in our country today is that we have accustomed ourselves to a concept of an easy type of Christianity.

I was a young man when I first came from Europe to America. To me, this land was the fairest land in the world. From our early childhood, our Russian nurse had talked to us about America whenever she wanted to get our attention. She would tell us how beautiful everything in America was. She pictured to us chariots that had spokes and hubs of gold, and horses shod with shoes of gold. According to her stories, all the spoons and dishes in America were of gold. The first American I ever saw had gold teeth. So I was sure that in this land all the people had teeth of gold. What a wonderful fairyland America was to my imagination!

I came to this country from a land of persecution. It was a land of suffering and bloodshed. It was a land that saw many of its people banished from their homes. It was a land where men and women sealed their faith with their blood. I came to America and I was amazed and somewhat shocked to see the popularity which Christianity had gained in this country. There seemed to be a real absence of knowledge that discipleship and suffering can never be separated if one is to have a strong Christian character and testimony. The moment these are separated you find a wishy-washy concept of Christianity.

Suffering Is a Necessity to the Ministry

Examine again verse 10 of II Corinthians chapter 4 and add to it verse 11. "Always bearing about in the body the dying of the Lord Jesus, that the life also of Jesus might be made manifest in our body. For we which live are always delivered unto death for Jesus' sake, that the life also of Jesus might be made manifest in our mortal flesh." We cannot escape the fact stated in these verses that suffering is a necessity in the ministry.

In our last chapter we established the fact that in order for the vessels of the ministry to perform their particular purpose, they must reflect the glory and character of the indwelling Christ. The verses before us point out that in order to be able to reflect the glory of the indwelling Christ, suffering is a necessity. Look again at these phrases: "Always bearing about in the body the dying of the Lord Jesus," and "that (in order that) the life also of Jesus might be made manifest in our body." We carry in our bodies the dying of the Lord Jesus in order that His life might be seen in us.

It is important here that we establish the meaning of the word "life." It tells us that we have His life in our body. The body, of course, refers to our earthly tabernacle. The life of Jesus spoken of here is the spiritual life, not the natural life. There are two expressions in the Greek language which are translated life. One is "psuche," which refers to the natural or bodily life. It is used in such a passage as John 10 where the Lord said, "I lay down my life for the sheep." There the word "life" is psuche. A second word, however, is the

53

word "zoe." This word speaks of the spiritual principle of life, not of the bodily life. In the passage before us in II Corinthians it speaks of the manifestation of the spiritual glory of Jesus Christ in our bodies.

Before Christ can be seen in us, we must die. "Always bearing about in the body the dying of the Lord Jesus." So then, in order that this manifestation of life might be possible, we must discipline and deny self. Our human nature as such requires self-denial and suffering in order that the life of Jesus Christ might be magnified within us. The very structure of our human nature is such that there will be only a limited reflection of the glory of Christ, save only as we are subjected to serious suffering and hardships.

Some time ago while in Japan, one of our missionaries informed me of a very interesting establishment. It is owned by a Japanese Christian who is a rich man because he has been successful in producing pearls. I had him explain to me how it is that the beautiful pearl which he showed me was produced.

The men in his line of business drag the bottom of the sea in order to find a certain kind of snail. When found, they are taken into the laboratory and, with the use of a very sharp knife, the fishermen pierce each snail at the most sensitive part of its nervous system. Into that wound, they insert a little kernel of sand. Then they close up the wound, put the snail in a bag from which it cannot escape, and put it, with the others which have been treated likewise, into the depths of the sea. There they remain for a number of years.

These bags are all numbered, and the Japanese pearl fishermen know where they are and when to fish them out again.

This point of irritation introduced into the most sensitive part of the anatomy of that little animal causes her to suffer. Because of that suffering she produces a certain fluid with which she surrounds the kernel of sand in order to protect herself from the hurt it has caused her. So through the suffering of the snail, and through the secretion that she makes, there comes a wonderful transformation to that grain of sand. Through this process it is changed into a beautiful pearl.

This Japanese Christian man explains that the more successful the fisherman is in piercing the center of the nervous system of the snail, the better will be the pearl produced. The greater the suffering of the snail, the more beautiful the pearl.

When I read this passage in God's Word, I thought of the pearl industry in Japan. Do you know that the "pearls" in the great household of the kingdom of God can only be produced under the pressure of tremendous suffering? If you have not in your Christian life come to recognize that suffering plays its part in your spiritual development, you have missed an essential truth. You will never be counted among the precious pearls of the glorified Christ if such suffering is either denied us, or we are not exercised by them.

These sufferings may vary. There may be suffering of actual pain by the body. There may be sufferings of one kind or another brought on by circumstances. Perhaps some are due to persecutions. Whatever the reason, let us recognize that the glory of the image of Christ will not be seen in the bodies of believers, save only as they pass through suffering.

Yet for some reason or other we want to rebel against God when hardships face us. We do not want such suffering. We rebel when oppositions are met. Our hearts rebel when we meet obstacles. We rebel against the limitations which come our way in the ministry. We forget that we are actually going against the very things that will produce the quality of life God wants to see in us.

What today is one of the greatest problems in the Christian ministry? What is the greatest problem in our missionary enterprises? The problem is that our Christian service is determined by the extent we can do it without any serious sacrifice on our part.

Today so many Christians feel that what they do is dependent on what returns they may get in one way or another. With what we speak of as full-time Christian workers the matter is about the same. We are gratified that we serve the Lord, but on top of that we want to have the pleasure of being comfortably and well-provided for. If such provision is not made, then we do not feel obligated toward the service. May God redeem us from such a deceptive concept of Christian work.

Let me put it this way. How many of what we call full-time Christian workers would stick out their work through a great financial crisis in which they remained unpaid for a month or two? They might have to eat dry bread instead of the good meals to which many are accustomed. Let us investigate with honesty the motivations of our ministries. If it is a ministry unto the Lord, then it is done irrespective of any outward compensations. Our ministry is carried on in relationship to our Master and is not subject to outward circumstances, no matter how difficult they may be, how financially trying, or how physically hard they prove to be. We stand before God as the One to whom we minister; and we suffer in our body in order that our ministry may be acceptable and that the glory of the life of Jesus might be manifested through these bodies of ours.

Suffering Is Our Greatest Benefit in the Ministry

Our ministry is measured by our relationship to the hardships and trials and testings which our ministry brings with it. This in the wisdom of God is brought home to our minds and hearts in one way or another.

A missionary executive was getting ready to leave for a four or five months absence in a ministry on the African continent. To be absent from his family for any length of time was never easy, but this time, it was especially hard for his youngest boy felt so keenly the coming separation. As the father packed his suitcase the boy came to him and said, "Daddy, do you have to go?"

He said, "Yes, son, I have to go."

"But Daddy, you will be away for so long." He wept as he said, "I will have no Daddy. Must you go?"

"Yes, son," his father answered, "I must go." Then he tried to explain by saying, "The Lord

Jesus wants me to perform this ministry."

The boy then asked, "Daddy, does He want you to do it even if I have to stay here at home, and we have no Daddy here?"

"Yes" replied the father, "He wants me to do that."

"Daddy," he said, "if I die while you are gone, will you come back to the funeral?"

"No, son," was the reply. "I couldn't come back for your funeral because I would be too far away."

He went into the other room and wept, saying to his mother, "Daddy is leaving, and if I die he won't come back to my funeral."

The father could not bear that, so he had another talk with him.

In the railroad station, the little chap put his arms around his father's neck. When the train came roaring into the station, the boy's arms drew closer and closer around the father. "Daddy," he said after taking a deep breath, "you have to go, don't you?"

"Yes, I want to go because of Jesus," was the reply.

"If you do it for Jesus . . . if you do it for Jesus . . . then it must be hard, must it not?" he asked.

The father answered, "Yes, son, then it must be hard."

At last he released his father and said, "Daddy, I want you to go," and kissed him good-bye. The father boarded the train, but did not sleep much that night. Again and again his son's words kept ringing in his ears, "Daddy, if it is for Jesus, then it must be hard."

How hard? Not from the standpoint of motivation, but from the standpoint of discipline and suffering. But this is all so that the glory of our Lord may be magnified in our mortal bodies. Suffering, then, in conjunction with the ministry, is not incidental, it is a necessity. It is in suffering that God demonstrates the marvelous supernatural character of the spiritual life in the believer. What has been the most fruitful eras in the history of the Church? It has been the eras of suffering. It has always been the blood of martyrs that has been the seed of the Church.

Recently when traveling through Rome, I stopped at the great amphitheater Nero had built and where thousands upon thousands of Christians had gone singing to their death. There they were torn alive by wild beasts; but while the Christians died, the people in the galleries were accepting the Lord Jesus Christ. Instead of exterminating Christianity, the persecution spread it like wildfire throughout the entire Roman empire. It was in the midst of this suffering that the marvelous, supernatural power of the Christian Church was demonstrated.

Why is it that the message today in America has so little effect? We have substituted the fruit of suffering with the appeal to the spectacular. We think that gadgets, and all kinds of advertising, with overstatements concerning speakers that come to our pulpits, will attract the people. Seemingly all the sensational advertising that we have attached to Christian service today has not brought the grip of the supernatural power of the gospel upon the people of our generation. Why has this come about? Because our present message is born in circumstances of ease and luxury and intellectualism instead of being born in the trials and testings and sufferings and anxieties of a living, witnessing, suffering Church. This is the reason for the impotency of the message of our day in our beloved America.

I have seen something entirely different, however. How is it that today behind the Iron Curtain the Church is growing by leaps and bounds? Meeting places are closed again. For a very brief time there was a greater liberty in Russia which deceived some. But does lack of religious freedom hinder the cause of the Lord? No, the Church goes on. The reason is that through the sufferings of God's people there is a demonstration of the supernatural life that God has placed in the hearts of His people.

Let us re-establish our faith in this unchanging truth: "When we cease to bleed, we will cease to bless." Here is the answer to the impotency of the Church of Jesus Christ in our blessed America. It has little suffering to bear. It does not face persecution. Men can be in the Christian ministry and live well. This, of course, is not true of all, but the point is that in many cases no self-denial is made, and that is why the power of the message is gone.

The Benefits of Suffering

The Apostle Paul takes up the subject of the benefits of suffering in verses 13 through 15 of II Corinthians 4. "We having the same spirit of faith, according as it is written, I believed, and therefore have I spoken; we also believe, and therefore speak; Knowing that he which raised up the Lord Jesus shall raise up us also by Jesus, and shall present us with you. For all things are for your sakes, that the abundant grace might through the thanksgiving of many redound to the glory of God." In verses 13 and 14 Paul points out how God is establishing our faith. It is through testings that it is grounded and strengthened. In our land of plenty and comfort there are few things to test our faith.

My childhood and youth were very different from many standpoints. I was privileged to pass through the 1920-'21-'22 starvation years in Russia. Millions of people fell like flies about us. Those were also years when God's people suffered for their faith. I am glad that I was a witness to the suffering of men of God who were put in prison and were tortured, but stayed true to our Saviour. Some of my closest friends in the days of my youth gave their lives to the cause of the gospel. The Lord spared me and brought me to America, but as I think back over those times of great suffering, I have found my faith strengthened through the testimony and witness of those men of God who gave their all for Christ.

My father was an evangelist during those years and found it necessary to travel a great deal. An urgent call came to him at one time to go to Siberia because so many persons there did not know the Lord. He decided to go, but that left us at home with some very serious problems. We were not provided with bread or with necessary clothing. Father would be away for months, and we would have to struggle along as best we could. One evening Mother said to him, "I cannot believe that this is God's will because you do not even have clothes to put on in order to go to Siberia. You have only one suit, and that suit is old and patched on your elbows and knees."

We have not seen preachers in America with patches on their knees. Perhaps there would be more power if they had. But there were many such preachers in my country in those days. One of my sisters who has a wonderful singing voice sat down one evening to play a guitar as this situation came to a crisis. The family was weeping, and she sang in the Russian language the song, "His eye is on the sparrow, and I know He watches me." That song made such an impression upon us that my father suggested, "Let's kneel down and thank the Lord that He will make provision for us all." We knelt down and asked that if God wanted my father to preach in Siberia He would make provision for clothing and for food for all of us.

The next morning a man came through our village with a number of army blankets which he had received from the American Relief Society. The Spirit of God led him to leave those blankets at our house. That was just two days before my father was to leave for Siberia. They provided cloth for the needed suit, and the kind of suit that was needed for Siberia. Some of God's people got together and worked during the day and into the night in order to get that suit ready. But that was not all. A woman whose husband had died came to our house with a fur coat left over from the olden days. She felt led of the Spirit of God to bring that fur coat to our house.

My father decided to go believing that the Lord would provide for our needs. The day after he started for Siberia a man came from a distant point with a cow and left it at our house, so that we would have milk. Provision after provision was made. We were amply taken care of.

It was through such suffering that we experienced the providing grace of God. It is in suffering and in testing that our faith grows, and through that we are established and rooted.

But we need not wait until persecutions come before our faith can be established. The Lord himself says, "He who wants to follow me, let him take up his cross and follow me." He also said, "Let him deny himself." The soundness of our Christian faith will be established as through self-denial we experience more fully the communication and manifestation of our God and His interventions in our behalf.

It is through suffering that the abundance of His grace is manifested as we read in verse 15, "All things are for your sakes." How can God manifest to us the sufficiency of His divine grace if we do not have suffering in our ministry and for our testimony? Why is it that Romans 5 tells us we glory in tribulation? The reason is that tribulation works patience, and patience experience, and experience hope, and hope will not let us be ashamed. These, then, are the blessings of hardship and suffering in the ministry.

There is one further step that verse 15 brings

before us: "That the abundant grace might through the thanksgiving of many redound to the glory of God." God wants not only that we should have an abundance of grace, but that through the grace we have received, we shall bring others into the marvelous fellowship of our Lord. These also will give thanksgiving, which will redound to the honor of God, because they have been made recipients of the supernatural power of that grace which has been seen in us as we have suffered for Jesus' sake.

Let us go back to a question we have raised already. How is it that so few people are being saved through the ministry of the gospel in our day? We have the answer in the Scripture before us. The abundance of the grace of God has not been demonstrated sufficiently in the lives of those whom God chose to bring the reality of this salvation in Christ to the world around them. It is through suffering that the abundance of this grace is demonstrated. That grace is sufficient for all kinds of circumstances and will elicit from its recipients an expression of thanksgiving and praise that will redound to God's glory and honor.

Do not avoid the difficulties or the sufferings which accompany the gospel ministry. These very things are essential to the effectiveness of your witness. But when God allows many trials and difficulties and sufferings to come your way, do not act as a martyr. It is highly objectionable in Christian workers when they complain of the limitations they have taken upon themselves as being burdens. When someone in the full-time ministry tells me, "I could draw such and such a salary, but because I am in the Lord's work, I have to sacrifice that," I believe they have the wrong attitude toward their work. It would be better for them to re-evaluate their basic motive for being in the ministry.

Evaluate properly these tribulations and limitations that come upon you for the gospel's sake. It is through such disciplines that God can work through your life to bring honor to Himself. I have personally wondered if America can be helped without suffering. I wonder if there is no other help for the Christian testimony in our country than days of suffering—suffering for Jesus' sake.

Chapter V

THE TRIUMPH OF THE MINISTRY

The apostle presents the triumph of the ministry in these words: "For which cause we faint not; but though our outward man perish, yet the inward man is renewed day by day. For our light affliction, which is but for a moment, worketh for us a far more exceeding and eternal weight of glory; While we look not at the things which are seen, but at the things which are not seen: for the things which are seen are temporal; but the things which are not seen are eternal" (II Cor. 4:16-18). The work of God must culminate in triumph. The second chapter of this same letter to the Corinthians emphasizes this truth. We read, "Thanks be unto God, which always causeth us to triumph in Christ." Since it is the ministry of the living God it must result in glorious victory. It can never be otherwise.

The Possibility of Triumph

We must connect the phrase in verse 16: "For which cause we faint not," with the previous verse which says, "For all things are for your sakes, that the abundant grace (of our Lord) might through the thanksgiving of many redound to the glory of God." The assurance of that final triumph rests in the abundance of the divine grace. The provision God makes is sufficient. It is thoroughly adequate to meet the need.

As we analyze verse 16 we learn that because of this sufficient provision we need not faint. Thus the possibility of victory is presented to us through the fullness of grace. We are also told that though our outward man perish, yet the inward man is renewed day by day. So the possibility of the triumph rests in the daily renewal of the inward man and the perishing of the outward man.

It is common knowledge with us that our physical body is subject to continuous decay. Our body cells have to be constantly replenished through the food that we eat and its assimilation into the body. If we neglect that food it is not long before our strength fails.

This truth Paul well applies to the natural man in the Christian. The "natural man" must die just as the natural body must die. Paul speaks of a daily death when he says, "I die daily." Here he speaks of the constant discipline of life through which victory is gained over the "old man" and the spiritual life is renewed. This is a daily thing.

This fact is very important, for triumph is possible only on the basis of daily renewal.

The moment we seek the victorious manifestation of God in our lives in any other way, we will find that we lose the victory in the ministry. We are inclined to make our ministry dependent upon particular experiences where we seek to reach the summit of our Mount Tabors. But these do not prove sufficient. The Tabor experiences will give us additional perspectives, but they do not provide the daily renewal that must be experienced by us. The triumph in the ministry is dependent upon the daily provisions of God in our spiritual lives.

An illustration of this is provided for us in the Old Testament. When God led Israel into the wilderness and fed them with manna, He gave them only sufficient manna for each day. The only exception was the day preceding the Sabbath when He provided enough for two days. By this He emphasized the sanctity of the Sabbath. But what was His purpose in making provision for only one day at a time? Some of the Israelites found to their grief that if they gathered more than was necessary for one day, it would become infested with worms. By this method God made His people dependent upon Him for daily provision. With the exception just noted, they could not carry anything over from the previous day to help them meet the responsibilities of the second day. There had to be a renewal made every morning.

We live in a day of much theological training and preparation and specialization. In this country we have an abundance of helps in the preparation of messages and lessons. The Sunday school teacher can get a dozen books that will give him or her material to interpret and teach the Sunday school lesson. The average preacher can reach for a commentary and find an outline on practically any portion of the Scriptures. This is all very fine, but somehow within all this efficiency there remains an inward ineffectiveness which is cause for great alarm.

I recall the last time my father visited me in the study of the church of which I was then pastor. He spent quite a good deal of time going over the many books. He did not say much about them until one afternoon I asked him, after having returned from making some pastoral calls, "Father, what have you been doing all day?"

"Oh," he said, "I have been in your library."

I then asked him, "What do you think about it?"

He was quiet for some time, then said, "Son, I am concerned."

That expression struck me. I wanted to know why he was concerned.

He replied, "I am concerned lest the books you have take the place of The Book. I am concerned lest the many helps will lessen your dependence upon daily revelation from God."

I will never forget that statement. As good as all the specialized training in our day is, and as good as all the helps that we can get today are there is danger that they will take the place of The Book.

There is also the danger that through the routine of work we do not depend on a daily renewal of our fellowship and communion with God. We have perhaps greater eloquence and greater oratorical ability in the pulpit today than any other age or generation has produced, but in many cases the ministry is not triumphant. That comes only through the daily renewal of the soul in communion with God. Truth can be so well-known to us that we can give it out like a record player, but it remains ineffective for lack of that daily renewal with God.

What I am making reference to is more than an habitual reading of the Bible in order to quiet our conscience. It is more than finding a few points of interest and doctrine that we can emphasize and will fill up the time when we go before a Sunday school class. Renewal from day to day consists in a personal assimilation of the truths God has revealed in His Word through His Spirit, and which comes to us through personal fellowship with Him. That is the process of renewal. But it must be every morning, every day; there is no other way. This generation needs to be brought back to inward dependence upon the communication of God from day to day so that the privileges we have in our generation may not destroy the effectiveness of our ministry.

During my ministry in a large pastorate on the West Coast I was constantly laboring under a busy schedule. There are times when a pastor has to pull out the plug on the telephone in order to have quietness and get alone with God.

I had just been to a convention where I had preached before ministers and deacons. This did not give me adequate time for preparation for my Sunday morning message, and I sensed deeply as I spoke that I did not have the communication of power from above.

As was my custom I stood at the door and shook hands with the people as they left the church building. Some of the men said, "Pastor, what a wonderful sermon, what a wonderful sermon!" But there was an old mother who waited until all the people were gone. She came and I said, "Mother so and so, how are you today?" She looked at me, and she had some pearls in her eyes.

She said, "Pastor, I must pray more for you."
I asked, "Why?"

She said, "Your message was eloquent, but it lacked the unction of the sanctuary."

I walked out of that church and went into my study. I did not eat any dinner that day. A saintly woman had sensed the pastor was in need of the unction of the sanctuary.

It is that unction from day to day that the apostle is speaking of here. It is that unction of the sanctuary that makes the difference between failure and triumph in the ministry.

The Benefits of Afflictions

The apostle tells us that our light affliction which is but for a moment, works for us a far more exceeding and eternal weight of glory. We have already seen that there is a very distinct relationship between suffering and triumph in the ministry, and this verse adds the truth that these things work for us a great measure of glory.

There are difficulties and hardships in the ministry. There are some who translate the word for affliction here by the word "pressures." That is a common word in our present-day vocabulary. We speak of laboring under pressures which vary in their character and source. Pressures may arise from ill health, or misfortunes of various kinds; but whatever they are, whether outward pressure or inward pressure, they work for us an exceeding great measure of glory.

We commonly think of afflictions as a hindrance in the triumph of the ministry. Yet here we learn that afflictions can lead to glory in the ministry. We look at obstacles and pressures and find ourselves saying that these are hindrances and are the reasons why we cannot be effective in our ministry. But this verse helps us look at them from the right standpoint. We must evaluate them by looking at them from the proper angle. These things, as does tribulation, work for us.

Some years ago I stayed with a family while in a revival meeting. On the Saturday there was no service in the church but there was a wedding. The father, mother, daughter, and son all went to the wedding; but I stayed home on the farm in order to prepare the messages for the next evening. When they returned I questioned them with regard to their impressions of the ceremony.

The father was greatly impressed by the message the preacher gave. The mother, on the other hand, was emotionally disturbed because she realized that soon she would be attending the wedding of the last of her daughters.

I then asked the daughter what she thought about the wedding. She said, "Brother Toews, you should have seen that beautiful bride," and she described her with the vocabulary that only a bride-to-be could use.

Lastly I went to the boy who was a lad of about ten or eleven. I said to him: "Jack, were you also at the wedding?"

"Yes," he said, "I was there."

"How was it?"

"Oh, boy," he said, "they had some wonderful cookies and cake." That was his impression of the wedding.

Such a variety of evaluations is possible to anything that takes place in our experience. So it is with reference to the various afflictions that come to us; our attitude toward them is entirely dependent upon our viewpoint concerning them. This we must clearly see: in the Christian ministry —and this is a fundamental aspect—the afflictions, the difficulties, the obstacles that come our way all work for us to the triumph of the ministry. Those very things that we so often think are unfortunate and exert upon our lives the greatest pressures, are the means through which God develops us and causes us to depend constantly upon Him.

I depended a great deal upon the wise counsel of my father. Whenever I became discouraged in the pastorate, I would go and tell him everything about my troubles. On one occasion I said to him, "Dad, I don't know that I can stay long with that church." I told him of one person who was a constant irritation to me and of an officer in the church who refused to cooperate. As I poured out my heart to him I said, "Why should I continue to work with people who make such pressures upon one's ministry?"

He listened very quietly to what I had to say. Then he said, "Son, do you know that the obstacles in the ministry are the secret of your making?"

That is exactly what the Apostle Paul means when he says that *our light afflictions which are but for a moment work for us.* The pressures of the ministry work for us an exceeding and an eternal weight of glory. It is through them that glory is being developed.

74

The days of the First World War and the revolution which followed were days of great poverty for us, and we had to do everything possible in order to keep alive. We raised silk worms—thousands upon thousands of them. It was responsibility to go to the large mulberry hedges and get the leaves on which the worms feed.

It was always an interesting process to me to see how the butterflies would emerge from their cocoons. They must put forth tremendous exertion in order to squeeze through the little hole in the cocoon. They sometimes struggle for a whole day, and it is a life-and-death struggle. When I saw them struggle so hard I decided that I would help them. I took a little pair of scissors and made the hole through which they were to come a little bigger. I was delighted over the large number of butterflies that were born in such a short time. But after a little while when my mother came and looked at them, she said, "What has happened? These butterflies can't fly. They will die."

Every one of these butterflies that I helped to emerge in an easy way from the cocoon could never deposit seed. They were all ruined. I learned a great lesson. My mother told me that it was the struggle through which they passed which made them fit for their purpose in life. If something was wrong with them they died.

And so it is with the pressures which we sometimes think will crush us. We forget that that is a process whereby we finally break through the limitations of the cocoon and are made able to triumph in the ministry.

Then if we will look upon these afflictions from

the standpoint of eternity as the apostle does in this particular case, we will see they are but for a season. Viewed in this larger perspective they are light, but they work for us a far more exceeding and eternal weight of glory.

So then, the process of our development and the degree of our usefulness and the spiritual depth of our ministry all depend upon these afflictions which come upon us.

I consider that one of the greatest tragedies of our generation is the absence of outward and inward pressures of a kind which will develop our youth in the proper way. All of our education and the advantages given our growing generation cannot make them measure up to the spirit and the capacity and manhood of our forefathers who came here as pioneers. Many of them had little education, but they had greater stature as men and women than most in our day, and that greatness resulted from the struggles through which they passed.

Today everything must conform to our rocking-chair philosophy. Everything must be easy for us and contribute to our comfort. But it is this very thing that produces softness. It is this very attitude that is responsible for the lack of stamina both spiritually and socially in our country today.

If you would examine the content of the Christian hymns you would find that most of them were born under affliction and tribulation. What was the secret of the great preachers of the past? They were the product of a melting process in the fires of affliction. Thus the triumph of the ministry rests upon the troubles which are brought upon us, because they work for us a degree of glory that far exceeds the trials through which we pass.

The Reality of the Triumph

The reality of this triumph comes to us in the eternal perspectives with which we view the ministry God has committed to us. "While we look not at the things which are seen, but at the things which are not seen: for the things which are seen are temporal; but the things which are not seen are eternal." We must again and again view the ministry and the hardships and difficulties of it from the standpoint of its final triumph. There are times when we feel the difficulties are such that we cannot carry on in the work any longer. Then is the time for us to look at the end result, and we will be encouraged to see the marvelous march of the purposes of God on their way to final completion.

Let me refer once more to those days of poverty and starvation and anxieties in Russia. We had no tractors then or horses. The wars had taken them all away. Some had a cow to plow with, and they were considered rich if they did. What cultivating we did was done with the spade and with the hoe. We planted our corn with a spade and cleaned the field with our hoe. We had only a very narrow strip of land, but the rows were quite long. It was a tedious job to hoe that whole section by hand. It took the whole family to do it. My father would hoe one row and I as the eldest son would take another. One of my sisters would take a third row, and the younger ones would come behind and pull the weeds that were close to the corn. For those young ones the rows were long. One of the boys found them especially difficult. He would always seek to lie down in the shade and then father would say, "Son, Up! Work!" But the boy would object, saying, "Daddy, it's such a long way to the end."

Then we had an idea. We made an agreement that every time we came to the end we would eat from a pot of cooked rice. It was cooked with water, not with milk, for we did not have milk. And the rice we received came from America.

So, when the boy would lie down in the shade, father would say, "Well, son, there is the kettle of rice."

The dear boy would always look (we were always hungry in those days, because we were undernourished), and then he would drive his weak body to pull some more weeds; and from time to time he would look to the end of the row to the kettle of rice. This would give him fresh courage and he would say, "Daddy, I'm coming closer."

When he finally reached the kettle he was given a little bit of the rice. So the prospect of the rice was always a source of courage and strength to him. This is but a homey illustration, but it helps us to see that in the ministry to which God has called us He wants us to look forward to the end of it. There we will be given a reward from His own hand.

Many people look forward to the reward when they will wear a golden crown or golden crowns. If I receive such I will not be able to wear them.

I am sure we will throw them down at the feet of our Saviour.

The reward I long for, though I do not know that I will gain it is this: when I come into the presence of my Lord I hope I can hear Him say, "You have been a good and a faithful servant. You have done what you could."

I believe that such a statement coming from Him would mean more to us than anything else. Perhaps you feel that your part in the ministry is so insignificant that it would hardly count. But the reward given will not be on the basis of our position or popularity or the extent of our influence. It will be based on the character of our inward dedication, and our faithfulness to the assignment that God has given us, insignificant though it may seem to be.

There is the triumph in the ministry. Are you happy with the possibility of that triumph? Remember it is made possible in the daily renewal through fellowship with God. It is accomplished in the process of suffering and sustained in the light of eternal rewards. Are you ready to accept the ministry God has assigned you and go on to glorious triumph in it?